YOUR PATH TO SALARY INDEPENDENCE

How Anyone Can Control Their Financial Destiny

Dr. David Kuo

PARTRIDGE

Copyright © 2023 by Dr. David Kuo.

ISBN: Softcover   978-1-5437-7361-3
           eBook   978-1-5437-7362-0

All rights reserved. No part of this book may be used or reproduced by any means, graphic, electronic, or mechanical, including photocopying, recording, taping or by any information storage retrieval system without the written permission of the author except in the case of brief quotations embodied in critical articles and reviews.

Because of the dynamic nature of the Internet, any web addresses or links contained in this book may have changed since publication and may no longer be valid. The views expressed in this work are solely those of the author and do not necessarily reflect the views of the publisher, and the publisher hereby disclaims any responsibility for them.

Print information available on the last page.

To order additional copies of this book, contact
Toll Free +65 3165 7531 (Singapore)
Toll Free +60 3 3099 4412 (Malaysia)
orders.singapore@partridgepublishing.com

www.partridgepublishing.com/singapore

CONTENTS

Dedication vii
About the Author ix
What this book is all about xi
Introduction xv

Chapter 1	Where do I begin? 1
Chapter 2	How to get started 14
Chapter 3	What do I buy? 25
Chapter 4	Choosing our shares 33
Chapter 5	Stock picking made easy - Income shares 41
Chapter 6	Stock picking made easy - REITs 50
Chapter 7	Stock picking made easy - What about bonds? 62
Chapter 8	Stock picking made easy - Growth shares 67
Chapter 9	Stock picking made easy - Value shares 74
Chapter 10	Index trackers 79
Chapter 11	Building a portfolio with trackers 84
Chapter 12	Building the portfolio from scratch ... 88
Chapter 13	Rebalancing the portfolio 94
Chapter 14	The finishing line 102
Chapter 15	50 dos and don'ts of the salary Independence fund 107

DEDICATION

This book is dedicated to my parents who taught me from a very early age that if a person cannot control their money, then they will never be able to control their life.

ABOUT THE AUTHOR

David Kuo is a scientist at heart. He read Chemistry at Imperial College London and went on to gain a PhD by investigating the transport of hydrocarbons through polymer membranes.

He admits that it wasn't the sexiest of topics. But he said it did give him an opportunity to play around with some of the first-generation personal computers of the 1970s, improve his machine-code programming skills, understand how microprocessors worked, and he even managed to make dry water in his spare time.

After graduation, David worked in the family business in Hong Kong before spending a seven-year stint as a turf accountant at Ladbroke in the heart of the UK's horse-racing scene in the West Country. He left the fast-money gaming industry to pursue something more sedate.... a career in the stock market.

At the turn of the Millennium - just before the implosion of the dot.com bubble - he joined The Motley Fool in London where he honed his skills in financial journalism, broadcasting, investing and market analysis.

His no-nonsense, straight-talking views could be heard on the BBC, CNBC, Bloomberg, Al-Jazeera, and Fox. He was a co-host on The Danny Baker "All Day Breakfast Show" on BBC London where he brought his unique take on financial matters every weekday morning. He wrote a column in The Independent on Sunday.

He went on to become Head of Personal Finance before launching The Motley Fool's Asian outpost in Singapore. With his grounding in UK broadcasting, David's views about financial matters found their way onto BBC World Television, CNBC, and radio stations such as BBC World Service and London's Talk Radio.

He wrote a regular column called A Fool's Eye View for Singapore's daily newspaper The Straits Times, and currently contributes to The Business Times under the banner "Diary of a Private Investor". He comments regularly on financial issues on regional TV network, CNA, formerly Channel News Asia.

In 2020, David co-founded The Smart Investor Singapore to continue his mission of helping private investors invest for themselves for the long term. He passionately believes that the best person to manage our money is ourselves, because only we can truly know what we want. He sits on the Singapore Exchange Investor Education Committee that promotes financial learning.

WHAT THIS BOOK IS ALL ABOUT

Investing is nothing more than delayed spending. If we can manage to resist the urge to splurge today, then we can afford to get something bigger and better tomorrow. But we need to control the temptation to whip out our wallets and, instead, invest our money carefully.

If we burn through everything we have today - and thanks to credit cards, we can even spend next month's money today - then we will have nothing left for tomorrow. In some cases, we could even end up with less than nothing tomorrow.

Just as investing is delayed spending, using credit cards irresponsibly, is spending tomorrow's paycheque today. What on earth are we going to do when next month arrives? Spend the following month's money? That's how debt piles up, and why many people cannot get on the road to salary independence.

That really is the essence of investing.... a big dollop of jam tomorrow rather than the instant gratification of a thin smear of strawberry preserve today. Investing is not about getting rich quickly, but instead it is about enjoying getting sustainably richer, slowly. At least, that's how I want you to think about investing.

In order to do that, we need to know where we are now, where we want to be at a future date, how we plan to get to our destination, and what we should do when we get there.

If you fail to plan, then you plan to fail

To reach our destination, we will need a plan - preferably a road map with clear signposts. This book will provide you with a guide to invest the right way that will lead you to salary independence, which, by the way, is not the same as financial independence.

Point is, we can never be totally financially independent, that is unless we choose to live on a desert island and spend our time fishing for our supper and plucking coconuts from trees.

Sounds really idyllic, doesn't it? But the romance could quickly wear off when we run out of recipes that require coconuts and fish. I can think of half a dozen off the top of my head, but that's about it. So, let's scrub the desert-island idea.

We can, however, reach a point where we are no longer entirely reliant on a monthly paycheque. We can only do that if we are truly salary independent. We can only make that dream a reality if we have the means to control our own financial destiny.

So, salary independence is about being able to choose for ourselves who we would like to work for, when and where we want to work, or if we even want to work at all. Does that sound good to you? It is empowering. It is liberating. It is healthy for our minds and bodies.

Salary independence is about choosing when and how we are going to receive our income. By being in control of our investment portfolios, we have the ability to shape our investments so they can deliver growth when it is needed, and to produce income when it becomes crucial.

No jargon. No gobbledegook

This book will help us become salary independent. It is jargon-free, which, by the way, is not the same as being dumbed down or light on detail. Far too often, books on finance are jam-packed with equations and slang.

You won't find the Gordon growth model derived from first principles here. Heaven only knows why anyone would even want to try to do that. But you will find out how to put together a robust portfolio of shares that could deliver income and growth based on Myron J. Gordon's principles.

On that point, my former editor at the Motley Fool in the UK, Martin Wake, gave me a valuable piece of advice when I was submitting my first piece of writing.

He said that when writing about finance, the article should be easily understood by my son and daughter who were in primary school at the time, and my mother and father. It should never be a treatise to show off how much I know about finance.

I have taken his advice to heart. Far too often, financial experts wrap themselves up in gobbledegook. Not here. This book will break down the jargon into easy-to-understand concepts that will give you the confidence and courage to go it alone afterwards.

Truth of the matter is that investing is not hard. Anyone who can add, subtract, multiply and divide should be able to invest on their own, manage their own portfolio, and achieve their dream of salary independence.

INTRODUCTION

If you have got this far, then it means that you have read the earlier sections about me, and why I have written this book, and how it can help you.

If you haven't, then please start there first. Not reading the first two sections is akin to assembling flat-pack furniture without checking the instructions.

We have only ourselves to blame when we discover that the drawers for our bedside table don't work because we have two left-sided rails instead of a left and a right. I've been there. I know what it is like. I don't want you to go through the same pain.

So, don't risk going off the rails. We shouldn't if we remember to just keep things simple.

That's more than enough preamble. Let's get cracking with the basic concept of investing.

Same but different

Have you ever wondered what is the difference between saving and investing? Some people might think that they are one and the same. They are definitely similar but at the same time they are quite different.

Saving is something we do to accumulate money for something we need in the near future. So, we save up for a holiday. We save money for a fancy music system or a flashy new gadget that we have set our hearts on.

Investing, on the other hand, is something that we do with money that we don't need for five years or more. So, we invest for our retirement. We start investing for our children's education on the day that they are born.

Why, you might ask, should there be a difference? Aren't they essentially the same thing? They are definitely similar. But there are two main reasons why they are not quite the same, too.

How to lose money

The first has to do with inflation, which is the rate at which the buying power of our money is being eroded through rising prices. If the rate of inflation is running at 2% a year, it means that $100 today, would only buy $98 worth of stuff in a year's time.

The fact that something will cost a couple of bucks more in 12 months' time is not going to be too life-changing. It is manageable, and probably not enough for us to lose too much sleep over. But it can become an issue over the long term, which is why it is important to invest the money into something that can keep pace with rising prices.

If we put $100 under our mattress today, it will only buy us $67 worth of goods and services in 20 years' time if the inflation rate is running at 2%. In 40 years' time, it will only be worth $44 in today's money. That is why the money should be invested into things that can keep up with, if not soundly beat, inflation.

Doing nothing with our cash is a probably one of the best and easiest ways to lose money. Another way is to put our jeans in the washing machine without checking the pockets first. If we have done it once, then we are unlikely to ever repeat the painful experience again.

What is this thing called inflation?

Many of us might think of inflation simply as rising prices. For instance, if a visit to a barber last year cost $10 but now costs $12, then that would be a price increase of 20% in a year.

Next consider a plate of food that used to set us back $5 but now costs exactly the same. We could infer that there has been no price inflation at all. Fantastic! But then we notice that the portion of rice is smaller, and instead of six pieces of chicken, there are now only five pieces.

In other words, we are getting less now for the same $5 that we spent previously. It might not be as noticeable as an in-your-face price hike. But it is still inflation. We call it shrinkflation.

The shrunken plate of chicken rice might not even show up in some governments' statistics, which can be another big bone of contention. Just because it isn't reflected in some official inflation data table doesn't mean that our stomachs won't notice the difference.

Thing is governments measure inflation by looking at how the prices of a carefully-chosen basket of goods and services change over time. Some things might go up in price, whilst other items might go down.

Mr Average doesn't exist

The good news is that the basket could provide us with a broad sense of how prices have moved overall. The bad news is that it is not a perfect barometer to gauge the rate of inflation for everyone.

Trouble is, not every person or every household will buy everything that is included in the basket. Some of us might buy more of the items that have gone up in price, but none of the things that have gone down. In other words, our personal inflation rate could differ markedly from the official average consumer-prices inflation rate.

That is the problem with averages. It can tell us something but not everything we need to know. Consider a person who puts his feet in a hot oven and his head in a refrigerator. By the way, please don't ever try this at home.

On average, the person should feel quite comfortable. But in reality, it could be very unpleasant. The poor guy might never be able to wear shoes, ever again.

Same goes for inflation. We are all individuals. Chances are none of us are average. In fact, I would hate to be called average.

So, a good exercise could be to make a note of everything we spend on a regular basis for, say, a couple of months. Keep that somewhere safe. Then perform the same excise over the same two months a year later.

Compare the expenditure then, and what we spend now. That should give us a better idea of our personal rate of inflation than the official rate.

This is not to say that the official numbers are wrong. It simply means that the concept of the average person is a myth. A convenient myth. But a myth, nonetheless.

Some home truths

I said there are two main differences between saving and investing. Here's the second. This is important. So, sit up straight and pay attention.

If we put $100 into a savings account, the $100 should always be there provided we don't take it out and spend it. In other words, we aren't risking anything by leaving our money in the bank.

The same can't be said of investing in the stock market. If we buy $100 worth of shares today, it could be worth less than $100 just minutes or days after we have bought them. Then again, it could be worth a whole lot more than $100.

It's not because we are jinxed if the shares go down, or that we blessed with the Midas touch if they go up. The market has absolutely no idea about who we are or what our motives are for buying a particular share. Quite frankly, it doesn't give a monkey's.

Point is, the value of our investment could go down as well as up. That's the way the stock-market cookie crumbles. Shares can be volatile. Very volatile at times. Consequently, we don't want to be putting our savings for an annual holiday into the stock market.

It's not going to be easy to explain to the family why their vacation to Europe will now be a staycation at home. As much as we would like to think that we are stock-picking geniuses, the stock market can be horrifyingly erratic in the short term.

Not all bad news

But here's the good news. As compensation for taking on the risk of investing in shares, not to mention the occasional stomach-churning, short-term, head-spinning volatility, we are rewarded with a higher return over the long term.

The operative term to take note of here is "long term". The equity-risk premium or extra return over a risk-free investment, such as leaving our money in the bank, should become more apparent the longer that we stay invested.

That is why we need to adopt a long-term view when buying shares. We also need to accept that some - hopefully not that many - of our investments may not always work out quite as expected. So, we shouldn't even attempt to put all our eggs in one basket.

Instead, we can build a portfolio of shares to help reduce some of the risk. If we get it right, then the portfolio could become a perpetual motion machine that could be capable of generating growth and produce regular income, which can be reinvested into more shares to generate more growth and even more income.

CHAPTER ONE

Where do I begin?

The beginning is always today (Mary Shelley)

The quote from Mary Shelley was deliberately chosen because she was the science-fiction author who created the Frankenstein character. As much as I enjoy horror movies, the last thing we ever want to happen is to see our dreams of salary independence turn into a nightmare because of a lack of preparation.

So, the first rule is to only invest with money that we won't need for five years or more. Remember what we said about the stock market being volatile? Well, the stock market can make fools out of all of us in the short term.

Thankfully, regular bouts of short-term weakness in the stock market are eventually followed by longer stretches of strength. However, if we want to enjoy the upside, we must also be able to tolerate the downside.

Unfortunately, nobody will ever tell us beforehand when those moments of market weakness will occur. We just know that they will happen. So, we need to be able to ride the rough with the smooth. We can't easily do that if we need to access our cash just when the market is down.

How long is a piece of string?

That was rule number one. Rule number two is to work out how much we need to invest. That might sound a bit like asking how long a piece of string is.

Well, not quite because someone, somewhere, has provided us with a rule of thumb to help us decide just how long that piece of string actually is.

The rule of thumb states that the proportion of our salary that we should put aside should be equivalent to half our age, if we haven't already started saving for our retirement. Surely, it can't be that simple. Well, hang on for a piece of breaking news…. it really is that simple.

Consequently, a 20-year-old should consider putting aside 10% of his or her salary. People who are 30 years of age should invest 15%, and 40-year-olds should be prepared to put away 20% or a-fifth of their salary.

The upshot is that it is certainly better to be younger when it comes to investing. If I only knew then what I know now, I could have attained salary independence a whole lot sooner. You can because chances are that you are probably much younger than I am.

So, what is behind the thinking of this ever-so-simple rule of thumb? Is it merely the musings of a crazy person?

There is definitely method to the madness. Younger people have the benefit of letting the stock market work its magic on their money for longer. As we get older, though, our investing time horizon becomes shorter. Consequently, we are forced to invest more to achieve the same result.

Meet Jack and Jill

Consider two people, Jack and Jill. No, they didn't go up the hill to fetch a pail of water. Well, they did, but not here in this book.

The two characters are separately thinking about their retirement. Jack is 40 years of age. Jill is much younger. She is only 20 years old.

Jill puts aside $1,000 every month into her portfolio of shares that could grow around 8% a year. She does that religiously for 20 years before deciding that it was time to take a career break.

What's more, she doesn't put any more money into the portfolio after that. By the time she is 55 years old, her portfolio could be worth $1.8 million.

Jack hasn't been putting any money away at all during his working life. Jack liked to enjoy the good life. Who can blame him?

But when he reached the ripe old age of 40, he really thought that he should pull his finger out and start doing something before it is too late.

Can you guess how much he would need to invest in order to amass the same amount as Jill, namely, $1.8 million, by the time he is 55 years old?

He would need to put away $5,400 a month for 15 years. That is over five times more than Jill had to invest to achieve the same lump sum.

Unless Jack is on a very good salary, it could be quite a stretch for him to reach that goal. In his desperation, he might even be tempted to take bigger risks with his money, which is never a good idea.

There's no time like the present

That is why it is important to start as early as possible. It can be tempting to delay because there are so many other things that seem to be far more pressing. However, the more we delay now, the more we will need to put away later on.

There is really no time quite like the present to get started. As they say, it is time in the market rather than timing the market that counts. So, stop making excuses.

The longer that we leave our money to work in the stock market, the more our money should grow. It is such a simple idea that it is really quite baffling why more people don't start investing sooner.

How much is enough?

So, how much do we really need to invest to achieve salary independence? Before we explore that question in more detail, there is a wonderful story about a successful entrepreneur who is on a weekend break in a small fishing village. He happens on a fisherman who is sitting on a jetty staring out into the ocean.

The entrepreneur asks the fisherman why he isn't out at sea catching fish. The fisherman replied that he has already hauled his catch in the morning, and now he is enjoying the scenery.

The entrepreneur politely points out to the fisherman that he is not making full use of his assets. He tells the fisherman that he should consider hiring out the boat, and with the rent collected, he could eventually buy another boat and employ more staff....

.... before long, he could have an entire fleet of boats and a whole team of fisherman who could be working for him. He would have plenty of free time and lots of money, too.

The fisherman scratches his head and asks the entrepreneur how he should spend all the free time that he will have available to him. The entrepreneur tells the fisherman that he can do whatever he wants.... he could even sit on the pier and stare out into the ocean if he wanted.

The fisherman then asks the entrepreneur how is that any different to what he is already doing now!

So, how much is enough?

So, how much will we need? Please just put me out of my misery now. What is the magic number? How much do we need before we can tell the boss to take his unreasonable requests and shove it where the sun doesn't shine?

The amount will be different for everyone. There is no one-size-fits-all retirement pot.

Some might say that flying first class and staying at a five-star hotel four times a year is their idea of a modest family holiday. Their concept of dressing down could be a pair of Gucci loafers, Ralph Lauren slacks and the latest Lacoste t-shirt. Let's not forget the 24-carat gold chain and medallion around the neck, too.

Others might have more modest requirements. So, what we need to do is estimate our annual expenditure. That, by the way, is not the same as how much we earn. It is how much we spend in a year.

And we need to be really honest with ourselves here. The only person we will cheat will be ourselves if we aren't completely truthful.

Let's, for argument's sake, say it is $50,000 a year. For some people, that might be a fortune. For others it could be a tiny drop in a bucket. But let's just stick with $50,000 for now. It's so much easier to work with nice round numbers.

Don't forget that the $50,000 is in today's money. If inflation is running at 2% a year, then you could need twice that amount, namely, $100,000, in 30 years' time.

The 4% Rule

So, how much would we need to be able to generate $100,000 of income a year in 30 years' time? Guess what? There is yet another rule of thumb that could help. Simply multiply the required income by 25 to get the answer.

Why 25? It will become crystal clear in a moment.

So, if we want to generate an income of $100,000 a year, then we would need an investment pot that holds $2.5 million. With two-and-a-half million dollars in the portfolio, we should be able to safely withdraw $100,000, which is 4% of the nest egg, without ever having to eat into the capital.

That's because a nest egg that is properly invested should easily grow at more than 4% a year. It means that the amount that we take out every year should be comfortably less than the rate at which the nest egg will grow.

We should also be able to increase the annual drawings roughly in line with inflation without worrying too much about running out of money whilst we are still around to enjoy it.

So, what could that 4% rule mean for our friends, Jack and Jill with their $1.8 million nest eggs? They could, if they want, withdraw $72,000 when they celebrate their 55th birthday. What's more, they don't have to worry too much about exhausting their nest egg.

But if they want their yearly withdrawals to keep well ahead of rising prices, then they will need to invest the money in some really good inflation-beating assets.

Not so fast

So, you are itching to get going. You can't wait to start building your million-dollar portfolio. Who can possibly blame you? But hold your horses for a moment. There are a couple of things we need to think about first.

Remember what we said right at the start of this chapter: we should only invest with money that we won't need for at least the next five years. That should also include repayments on outstanding loans.

I know exactly what you are going to say. How is it possible to pay off all our outstanding debts? If we have to wait until all our loans are paid off, then we will never be able to start investing until it is too late.

It would be like trying to untie a knot of Gordian complexity. But just as Alexander the Great managed to slice through the knotty problem with his sword, we can do the same, too.

So, here's the thing: not all debts are alike. Credit card debts are outrageously expensive. The interest rates charged on outstanding credit-card balances can be eye-wateringly high.

The Exorcist

I am no apologist for credit-card companies, even though I do have investments in a couple of them. But I can understand why they have to charge the high interest rates that they do. It's because credit-card loans are unsecured. There is very little that card companies can do to us if we should default on our repayments.

Mortgage debt, on the other hand, is different. It is cheaper because it is secured against a physical asset, namely, our homes. If we are unable to meet our mortgage repayments, in other words if we default on our commitments, then our lender could foreclose on the property.

In the UK, it is called repossession, which sounds like something out of The Exorcist. Foreclosure? Default? And now repossession? It's enough to make our heads spin.

The term repossession perfectly explains what is happening. We never actually own or possess our home until we make the final mortgage payment to our lender.

So, the two types of debt are not the same, even though they are both considered as borrowings.

Before we invest, we should definitely make sure that we don't have overdue balances on our credit cards. We should also make sure that we can comfortably meet the monthly repayments on our home loans.

A simple trick

It goes without saying that whilst we are paying off our overdue credit-card balances, we shouldn't be making any more purchase until we get that debt fully under control. One useful trick is to literally put a freeze on our card.

We can put the card in a bag of water and put the whole kit caboodle in the freezer. We can still access the card in case of an emergency. It just takes a little time for the ice to thaw.

But that's the whole point behind freezing the card. It won't damage the card, but it will stop us from making impulse purchases, if we are someone who easily gives in to temptation.

Two sides of the same coin

Still not convinced. Think of it this way: if we have outstanding credit-card debts whilst we are investing, then we are effectively borrowing money at 20% or more a year to generate an annualised return of about 8% on the stock market.

By the way, the 8% investment return is not guaranteed. But the 20% interest rate on the loan probably is.

Borrowing money at a high rate of interest to generate an investment return at a lower rate just doesn't make good financial sense. Or as Dr Spock on Star Trek would say: That is completely illogical, Captain.

Let me quickly explain why. Let's say we borrow $1,000 on our credit card to invest in shares that could grow 8% a year. Let's also assume the minimum amount payable on the card is 2% of the outstanding debt, and interest is charged at 25%.

It will take roughly seven years to clear the credit card bill. Over that period, we will have made $1,839 in total repayments. If we had, in the meantime, put the $1,000 in the stock market, then provided there are no hiccups along the way, the investment could have turned into $1,713.

So, we have effectively paid $1,839 to make $1,713. It would be like trying to run up a down-escalator. It's not an enjoyable exercise. It normally ends up in failure.

So, pay off any high-interest debts completely. Then, and only then, consider investing in the stock market.

Remember that investing and paying down debt are effectively two sides of the same coin. Every dollar that is used to pay down debt that carries an interest rate of 20% a year is a guaranteed return of 20% per annum on our money.

It is hard to think of any investment that can promise that kind of return. There aren't. At least not many I can think of that are legal.

Admittedly, the bigger the risk we take, the bigger the return we could achieve. But some risks just aren't worth taking, regardless of what the promised return might be. Here is something that might be able to help us decide what a good investment should look like. Brace yourselves. It's another Rule of Thumb.

The Rule of 72

The Rule of 72 is often used as a quick way to determine how many years it will take to double our money if we know what kind of returns we can expect from an investment. We simply divide the projected annualised return into 72.

An investment that could deliver a return of 2% a year would take 36 years to double. An investment that delivers a return of 8% would theoretically take nine years to double.

But beware of investments that promise outstanding returns. They are either outright scams or extremely risky. Remember the old adage: if something looks too good to be true, then it probably is.

It is far better to opt for something that can deliver a modest but sustainable return rather than some get-rich-quick scheme. However, it shouldn't be so modest that would make it completely meaningless to invest any money into it.

CHAPTER TWO

How to get started

Eighty per cent of success is showing up. (Woody Allen)

By this stage we should have a pretty good idea about the differences between saving and investing. We should have a rough idea about how much we need to put away to amass our salary-independence nest egg.

We should also be aware that investing in shares might not always beat cash in the short term. Over the long run it should, though.

But what exactly are these things called shares? As the name suggests, it is a portion or a share of ownership in a business. We might own one share, 100 shares or perhaps thousands of shares in a company.

When we own shares, we immediately become shareholders or part-owners of the business. If the company does well, then we should also participate in its success. If it does badly, then we could feel the pain, too.

But here's the thing: we can't lose any more money than the amount that we have invested. Even if the company should implode spectacularly, the most that we can ever lose is limited to the amount that we have paid for the shares.

What's the downside?

Companies are limited by liability. In a nutshell, our liability as a shareholder is limited to the capital originally invested. Our personal assets are protected if the company that we have invested in should go bust, no matter how dramatically it collapses.

If we buy $1,000 worth of shares, and if the company fails, then all that we could lose is $1,000. That's it. Nobody can come to our house and take away our prize stamp collection or rifle through our drawers.

But any money that we have invested could be lost forever. That's the downside. The good news, on the other hand, is that the upside to buying shares is unlimited, if the company should do fabulously well.

So, those are the two extremes to investing. If we buy shares in good companies, then we could make an unlimited amount money for a very long time. But if we buy shares in bad companies, then we could lose our investment should the company go belly-up.

That can happen, which is why investing in shares is not risk-free.

That said, some companies have rewarded their shareholders for decades. They could continue to do so for many more years to come, too. The secret, therefore, is to invest in good companies and keep well away from the terrible ones.

By the way, it's not really that hard to find good companies, provided we know what to look for. More about that later on.

So, what do you think? Do you have what it takes to buy your first share? Of course, you do. You might even have an idea or two about which shares you might want to buy first.

How to buy shares

For the vast majority of us mere mortals, we will buy our shares on stock exchanges through the help of brokers. In ye olden days, we would phone up a broker to execute our orders by finding a suitable seller. Telephone brokers still exist.

However, most of us will now buy and sell shares on the internet. It is more efficient, probably faster, and very likely to be cheaper than talking to someone on the other end of a phone line.

These days, there are even brokers who will charge customers nothing to execute their orders. That's right, zero-commission brokers.

How on earth is that even possible? Why would a company provide a free service to customers? Do these saints walk around the stock exchanges with haloes around their heads? Don't they say that there is no such thing as a free lunch?

A stringy lunch

That is absolutely correct. There are no free lunches, especially in the financial world. Unfortunately, free lunches generally have strings attached to them. And there is nothing more unappetising than a stringy lunch. I've had a few of those in my day. I always ask for my money back.

So, where's the catch?

There is an old saying that if we are not paying for a service then we are not the customer. And that is precisely what happens at zero-commission brokers. Put another way, whilst the broker is, admittedly, buying and selling shares on our behalf, we are not actually the customer.

So, who is? Who benefits when the broker is executing our orders for nothing?

When we place an order to either buy or sell shares through our saintly and very generous zero-commission broker, it is sent to a third-party - a market maker - who actually compensates the broker for access to the trade.

So, our broker is acting more like a middleman between us and some other trader, rather than between us and the stock exchange.

These middlemen, therefore, are paying for information about not only our trades but the thousands of other trades that are taking place in the market. That helps them gain valuable insights into what is going on, and what might happen in the market, before us.

Is that really such a big deal? Probably not if we are long-term investors. But it's not great for frequent day-traders who like to think that they can somehow predict the direction of share prices.

What they don't quite realise is that they are merely puppets dangling on the end of a string. There's that blasted string again.

Market makers with their fancy black boxes are able to buy shares faster than the blink of an eye - long before our trades have even been executed.

Resist the urge

We shouldn't get too hung up about what happens behind the scenes at brokerage firms. After all, it is competition in the industry that is helping to bring down the cost of buying and selling shares, which is altogether a good thing.

What we do need to bear in mind is that just because it costs less (or even nothing) to trade, it doesn't mean that we should do it more frequently. That is precisely what these zero-commission brokers want their customers to do. The more we trade, the more they earn from those middle-men.

But brokerage commission is just one of a number of costs that we should try to avoid. For instance, there's stamp duty that needs to be paid on share purchases.

Another inescapable cost is the difference between the buy and sell price of a share. The buy or bid price is the maximum amount of money a buyer is willing pay for a share. The ask or offer price is the minimum of money a seller is willing to accept.

The difference, which is known as the spread, is one way that market makers make money. The ask price is always higher than the bid price. The spread between the two is ultimately a cost, which can be easily avoided if we just minimise our urge to trade.

It can be a much better idea to keep hold of our shares after we have bought them and enjoy the benefits of being a shareholder.

So, what exactly are these benefits?

Shareholder benefits

As a shareholder of a company, we are part-owners of the business. By the way, those rights don't extend to marching into the company's head office and settling down in the boardroom for a digestive biscuit and a cup of afternoon Earl Grey.

It does, however, give us an opportunity to have our say at the company's Annual General Meeting (AGM). We can do that by exercising our vote on issues that include the election of directors, the appointment of auditors, and the dividends that have been proposed.

The AGM is an important event in a shareholder's calendar. It only happens once a year, which is why it is called an Annual General Meeting. If you have any concerns about the company, then make sure your voice is heard at the AGM.

Don't ever be afraid to stand up for your rights. We are, after all, a part-owner of the company. If the business is underperforming, then we have every right to ask the directors why, and maybe give them a piece of our mind at the same time.

A load of knickers

I recall an AGM incident at a famous UK retailer that is renowned for the quality of its women's undergarments. The men's underwear is very good, too. I would never dream of leaving home without it.

At one particular AGM, an irate shareholder stood up and chided the directors for the disappointing lingerie on offer in the stores, whilst waving in the air a brassiere from a competitor. She wanted to know why, as a loyal shareholder of the company, she had to buy her unmentionables from somewhere else.

I can't comment on whether the range of lingerie has improved. But our job as shareholders is to hold directors' feet to the fire when it is deemed necessary. They are paid to do a job, which is essentially to look after the interest of shareholders.

If they fail to do their jobs, then we should let them know, in no uncertain terms.

Other benefits

The other benefit of being a shareholder is that we get to participate in the success of the business if it is doing well. We could be rewarded with a rising share price or a share of the profit in the form of dividends, or perhaps a bit of both.

Those dividends are generally paid in cash. However, some companies will give shareholders the option to take their dividends in the form of shares. It really depends on whether we need the cash or whether we would prefer to reinvest the money into more shares.

Some investors like to use the cash to buy shares in other companies that they already own. There is nothing wrong with that. It is called rebalancing the portfolio. But we will deal with that later on.

The ever-enlarging snowball

The important thing to remember is to reinvest any dividends we receive as quickly as possible. It is the principle behind compounding, which is a powerful way to grow our portfolios organically.

Think of it as a snowball that we roll along the ground when building a snowman. If snow isn't something that is common to your country, then substitute snow for a lump of dough. The analogy will work just as well.

Every time we receive dividends, we have three choices in front of us. We could spend the cash. And why not? It's our money and we can do with it as we like.

We could do nothing with it at all if we want. Just leave it sitting in a bank account until we find a good use for it. The danger with doing nothing is that the money could idle there for ages. Remember what we said about inflation?

If you are going to do nothing with the cash, then maybe it might be better to spend it. At least that way we might derive some immediate pleasure from the money. There is nothing wrong with instant gratification.

But remember what we also said at the start of this book - investing is just delayed spending, which is why I like the third option best of all.

If we don't need to spend the cash and we don't want to sit on the stuff, then consider putting it to work by buying more shares. Some companies will let us take our dividends in shares rather than cash. All we have to do is tick the box that opts for dividends in the form of shares rather than cash.

A lot to think about

We don't even have to take all the dividends as either shares or cash. We can choose what proportion to take as shares, and the rest will be paid as cash.

That is especially useful in some markets that still have minimum lot sizes.

Don't get me started on lot size. It is an archaic practice that should have died out with the dinosaurs. Unfortunately, in some markets, dinosaurs still exist. Trades can only be carried out in a fixed number of shares known as lots.

I have compared minimum lot sizes to a butcher who will only sell us one sheep at a time. It's ludicrous, right? What if we only want a couple of lamb chops for tomorrow's lunch?

It's even worse with shares because the price of each unit could be in the tens of dollars. Imagine having to buy 1,000 units of a share that costs $30 a pop. We could easily spend our entire allocation for shares on just one company.

It might be a fantastic company. But there are inherent risks with being overly concentrated on one company. We'll be delving deeper into diversification in the next chapter.

For now, we just need to know that in Singapore and Malaysia, the minimum lot size for buying and selling is 100 shares and multiples thereof. It was reduced from 1,000 shares.

In Hong Kong, each company can set its own lot size. So, check carefully before you trade.

In the UK and the US, investors can buy just one share, if that is all they want to buy. That's a good job and all. For example, one share of Warren Buffett's Berkshire Hathaway could set us back over US$400,000. We're not going too get many of those to the pound.

But be careful when buying small numbers of shares. We don't want to end up spending more on fees than shares.

CHAPTER THREE

What do I buy?

*If opportunity does not knock,
build a door* (Milton Berle)

So, you want to start buying shares. That's great. But with hundreds of thousands of shares available on numerous stock exchanges around the world, what should we buy first? Should we buy shares in just one company? No? What about shares in a couple of companies? How about three? Four?

So, how many different shares do we realistically need to buy for our portfolios? Okay, you can stop guessing now.

By now, we should have worked out how much we need to put into our nest eggs to generate the income that we need to be salary independent. In most situations, we won't have the entire sum of money available on day one.

So, we need to build up to it slowly. We also know how much we should be investing every year to reach our target by a certain date.

Let's use Jill as our case study. She plans to invest $1,000 a month for 20 years. In other words, she will be making 240 discrete monthly deposits into her salary-independence fund.

Ideally, she should be looking for around 20 good companies to invest in. There is nothing especially magical about the number 20. It is small enough for us to monitor how the various businesses are performing, and large enough so we don't put too many eggs into one basket.

Making a list

Start by making a list of at least 20 companies that you might be interested in. The longer the list the better. Not all of them will be able to make the cut. We'll talk more about screening later on.

For now, just assemble a list of possibles and probables. They could include shops that you like to visit or restaurants that you frequent. Anyone fancy a hamburger or a pizza?

They could be insurance companies that you use or perhaps your bank. What about your favourite supermarket or the developer that built your house? What about your favourite airline, or the hotel that you stayed at on your last vacation?

It shouldn't take too long to build a very extensive list of companies. But not all of them will be good companies to invest in. Nevertheless, it will get us to start thinking about the different types of businesses that are out there. It will remind us about just how diverse the stock market really is.

Believe me when I say that a trip to the shopping mall will never be quite the same again. We will start to look at products and services in a totally different light. A packet of fish fingers won't just be supper that night but rather a question as to who makes it, and could it be a good long-term investment for our portfolios?

Diversify or else

There is an old story about an ice-cream seller who does fabulously well when the sun is shining. On those glorious sunny days, he just can't stop making money. In fact, he has to replenish his stock of ice cream several times a day just to keep up with demand.

But when the heavens open up, he is hard pressed to sell even one ice cream cone. There is just no demand for ice cream when it is raining. Amusingly, his friend who sells not just ice cream but umbrellas, ponchos and kagools as well, is doing a roaring trade.

The moral of the story is to diversify. In other words, we should try to avoid putting all our eggs into one basket. As far as investing is concerned, it means buying into a broad range of companies in different sectors.

The key to diversification is totally different and unrelated sectors. So, buying 20 different banks is not diversifying. Buying 20 pharmaceutical companies is not diversifying. Buying 20 insurance companies is not diversifying.

Putting too much money into one particular sector could be just as risky as putting too much money into any one particular share.

Crash, bang, wallop

Some of us may remember the financial crisis of 2008. At that time, banks had lent money indiscriminately. They were shovelling heaps of money onto NINJAS. These are people with no income, no jobs, or assets to buy property that they simply couldn't afford.

Those loans were bundled together and sold to insurance companies and to consumers who wanted a reliable source of income. The idea was that the interest earned on the loans would be distributed to those investors as income.

Things were going swimmingly until some enlightened investors realised that the income from those bundled-up loans were far from dependable.

Then the penny dropped. It was quickly followed by the share prices of banks that collapsed over fears that they could go bust. It wasn't obvious at the time which banks were implicated or had been infected by the bad loans.

So, banks simply lost trust in each other. They stopped lending not just to consumers and businesses, but to each other, too. It was scary. Credit literally dried up overnight. Bank customers queued up at ATMs to withdraw their money over fears that their life savings could evaporate. Some banks did in fact go bust.

Consequently, it is important to make sure that we invest in a range of unrelated sectors. It might not be of much help if a tornado strikes. But if we haven't borrowed money to buy our stocks, then we can afford to batten the hatches, hunker down and wait until the storm passes.

Building a portfolio

So, building a diversified portfolio of assets is crucial. There are a couple of things to think about when building our portfolios. The first, and probably the most important consideration, is how much of our portfolio should we allocate to risk-free assets such as cash and bonds, and how much should we put into shares?

If we have too much in cash, then, whilst it is admittedly safer, it won't grow very fast. Remember what we said about the Rule of 72. If an investment is only growing at 1% a year, then it could take 72 years for it to double.

But we don't want all our money in risky assets either. What will we do if the stock market should crash when we are only a year or two away from the day we want to stop working? Heart-breaking wouldn't even begin to describe how we would feel.

So, how much should we allocate to cash and how much should we invest in shares? There is, believe it or not, a rule of thumb that could help us decide.

Rule of 100

The rule of 100 states that the percentage of our savings that should be allocated to shares should be equal to 100 minus our age in years. The rest can be in either bonds or cash.

So, on the day that a child is born, 100% of the infant's money should be put to work in the stock market. Someone who is 30 years old, should have 70% in the stock market and only 30% in cash and bonds. By the time we are 70, then only 30% should be in shares, whilst 70% should be in cash and bonds.

If we should live to 100, then congratulations. By the way, the chances of making it to 100 years of age is not nearly as remote as we might think. A 10-year-old child today has a 30% chance of being a centenarian.

I apparently still have a 10% chance of making it to 100. I sometimes wonder if I will be as cantankerous then as I am now.

By the time we make it to 100, then almost all our money should be in cash. Have you worked out why that should be the case? It's got nothing to do with older people being unable to follow what is happening in the stock market.

Instead, it has everything to do with stock-market volatility. Remember what we said about how the value of our shares can go down shortly after we have just bought them?

Crumble, correction, and crash

It can happen. In fact, shares can fall at any time, and sometimes for no apparent reason, whatsoever. Unfortunately, nobody can ever tell us when it will happen.

Some pundits would like you to think that they have been blessed with the gift of foresight. But they don't. The simple truth is that shares rise when there are more buyers than sellers. They fall when there are more sellers than buyers.

People buy and sell shares for all kinds of reasons, though. And those reasons aren't always logical. They might buy because of a fear of missing out when shares are going up. They might sell just because other people are selling.

The urge to follow what the crowd is doing can be overpowering. But if we aren't buying shares with borrowed money, then we don't need to worry. We can always afford to wait for sanity to return.

Problem is we don't know when common sense will return to the stock market. It could rebound immediately.

Then again, it might take weeks, months, or even years before people finally come to their senses.

Younger people have the luxury of time. Older investors, on the other hand, don't always have the same luxury. And that is why we should consider allocating less of our money to shares as we get older.

CHAPTER FOUR

Choosing our shares

I love the grey areas between right and wrong (Dan Brown)

We are now at the stage when can start assembling our portfolio of shares. But first a quick recap.

We should have some idea, by now, about how much we need to invest either as a lump sum or every month into our share portfolios. Remember we are aiming to buy shares in around 20 different companies that should be unrelated to each other.

The shape that I use to fit the 20 shares into is the pyramid. It is arguably one of the most stable structures known to man, with a sturdy base that tapers to a point at the very top.

Ideally, around 60% of the pyramid should contain our boring income shares. The middle 30% can contain our exciting growth shares, and the remaining 10% should hold our more speculative or value shares.

Huh? Income? Growth? Value? I thought you said this book was jargon free.

Don't worry. This is about as jargony as it gets. But it is important to appreciate that there are three basic types of shares in the market.

Knowing which share fits into which category will help us build a solid portfolio. It should help us sleep well at night, knowing that our pyramid should remain standing even if the market is ever badly shaken.

Boring income shares can be exciting

Income shares are companies that pay out most of their profits as dividends to shareholders. They were probably once exciting businesses that grew like the clappers.

But over time, they have slowed appreciably, and are now happy to just plod along doing the same old thing year after year.

Don't get me wrong. They are not unprofitable. Far from it. In fact, they can be very profitable. But it is because they don't need all the cash that they have generated that allows them to pay out most of their profits to shareholders in the form of dividends.

They can also grow a little, too. Not too quickly, though. But fast enough to increase their payout gradually. Think of them as the Volvos of the stock market. (Apologies to all Volvo owners). They will get you from A to B safely. Just don't think of them as head-turners.

In the main, these companies could grow at less than the rate that the market is growing. So, if the market grows on average around 8% a year, then don't expect these companies to grow any faster than that.

The reason for buying them is for the dividends that they can generate. They can spit out oodles of cash, which can come in handy for all sorts of reasons. We could use the cash to buy more shares, which, when added to the shares we already own, could mean more dividends next time around.

Christmas all year round

On that score, income shares can be quite exciting in their own way. There is nothing quite like hearing the sound of dividend cheques hitting our bank accounts at regular intervals.

Some income shares pay dividends every six months. Others pay them four times a year. If we have a portfolio of 20 shares, then it could almost be like Christmas every week of the year.

Another reason for buying them is to provide some stability to our portfolios. The market doesn't normally pay too much attention to income shares, which is another way of saying that they can be relatively inexpensive. Additionally, their share prices don't tend to swing around too much.

That is not to say that they are dirt cheap. Good reliable income shares can be quite sought after, especially when bank interest rates are low. The payout from these companies can be quite predictable, which is why some investors are willing to pay good money for them.

However, we don't want to go too far overboard with our income shares. Around 60% should be about right. We want to leave room for some growth shares.

Volvo vs Ferrari

If income shares are the Volvos of the stock market, then growth shares are probably the equivalent of Ferraris. They can go like the clappers, but they can also be quite high maintenance. They do need the right conditions to perform well. When those conditions are present, they can most definitely turn a few heads.

Growth shares can be expensive, though. Very expensive. That is because investors are paying up for the profit that these companies could make in the distant future, rather than what they can deliver now. Quite often they might be making little or virtually no profit at all today.

Nevertheless, investors are prepared to stump up good money for them now in the hope that these companies could turn into behemoths later on. Trouble is a lot can go wrong between now and later.

What if the expected rate of growth doesn't materialise? What if the competition eats into the growth company's market share? What if inflation should erode the company's future profit?

Plenty can go wrong with growth companies. But lots can go right too, which is why we should allocate at least some money to growth shares in our portfolios.

Too much of a good thing

If we have decided to assign around 60% of income shares to our portfolios, then roughly 30% could be used to buy growth shares. We don't want too much of a good thing, even though Mae West did say that too much of a good thing can be wonderful.

Thing is, Mae West wasn't talking about dividends. She was talking about something entirely different, which is really not a suitable topic to go into with a book on finance.

We, instead, are talking about dividends. And these companies don't generally pay a lot in dividends, if they even pay any at all. But some might. And those are the ones that we are looking to include in our portfolios.

In the main, growth companies prefer to use the cash that they have generated to grow the business. However, if we look hard enough, we should be able to find some good growth companies that also pay dividends.

What makes these particular companies interesting is that their dividends, albeit small, can grow quite quickly. That's because the company is bombing along at an eye-popping rate of knots.

So, don't be too dismissive about a low payout. Mighty oaks from little acorns grow.

If we earn, say, a dollar of dividends from a $100 investment, then that is equivalent to a dividend yield of 1%. That is pretty insignificant when our income shares could be paying four or five times more.

But if the payout could grow at 20% a year, that $1 could increase to $2 in just over three years, and double again to $4 in six years. There aren't many income shares that can do that.

Additionally, there is a pretty good chance that if the dividends are growing quickly, then the share price of the company might rise in tandem, too. And that is why the value of our portfolios could rise if it holds a decent spread of growth shares.

Speculate to accumulate

Some of you will have worked out that if 60% of the portfolio has been assigned to income shares, and 30%

to growth, then that still leaves 10% for something else. I told you investing wasn't that difficult.

So, what can we do with the rest of the portfolio that hasn't been invested in growth and income shares? This is where we can have a bit of fun with our portfolios. All work and no play makes Jack a dull boy.

If we have selected our income shares with care, and our growth shares with caution, then we can afford to look around for some slightly more speculative shares, such as value shares, to make investing more interesting.

So, what exactly are these value shares? The name should provide us with a bit of a clue. They are supposed to offer us value for money.

There are times in the market when some shares have been unfairly punished by investors. That could happen for a variety of reasons.

Every now and again, investors could suffer from a bad case of jitters. It could bring down the entire market, a sector within the market, or just specific shares. It is during those moments when some really good bargains can appear.

The market, we need to remember, is not as perfect as we would like to believe. It has a tendency to overreact.

It can be excessively enthusiastic, which can push up share prices to well above what they are really worth. Then again, investors can also be overly pessimistic.

When that happens, share prices can drop well below their true value.

The value investor is waiting for just those moments of market despondency to pounce. Their hope is that eventually the market could recognise the bargain. When that happens, the hidden value could be outed.

It could happen quite quickly, or it could take a while. So, the value investor needs to be patient.

Those, then, are the three main types of shares that we need to focus on. Income shares will provide us with lots of cash that can be used as we like. If we don't immediately need the cash, then it can be put to good use back in the portfolio.

Growth shares don't pay much in dividends. What they do pay, however, can grow quickly. That exciting growth rate can help to drive up the value of our portfolios.

Finally, value shares are there for their X-factor. These are ugly ducklings that have been ignored and dismissed by the market. But they could one day turn into beautiful swans.

CHAPTER FIVE

Stock picking made easy - Income shares

> *The only thing that gives me pleasure is to see my dividends coming in.* (JD Rockefeller)

I was once at a Singapore hawker centre standing in line at a stall holder who is famous for just one dish, namely, his excellent Char Kway Teow. That's all the hawker serves. But diners would still queue up patiently because they know that it would be well worth the wait.

In front of me was a tourist. He must have heard through the grapevine about this hawker's prowess to turn humble rice noodles in his flaming wok into one of the most delicious fares in all of Singapore.

After a 30-minute wait, it was the tourist's turn to be served. The hawker gestured to him with a toss of his head. The tourist who was evidently at a bit of a loss asked to see the menu. The hawker, with perspiration pouring off his forehead, raised one eyebrow and barked: "With chili or no chili?"

And that essentially is the choice that we have with the shares that go into our portfolios. Do we want the dividends to grow at a fiery pace, or would we prefer something a bit blander?

Show me the money

We should always try to remind ourselves that the lifeblood of our salary-independence portfolio is income. There will be times when we might lose our focus. This can happen when markets are in turmoil and share prices could fall sharply.

Those are the times when we must redouble our efforts to focus on dividends. Nothing else should matter to us, regardless of how much share prices might drop.

Consequently, every share that goes into our portfolios must reward us for holding it. They must be able to show us the money. They must pay dividends.

Some shares could pay copious amounts of dividends. Those dividends might not grow very fast, though. But that is still alright. Money is still money.

Some shares might not pay us much in the beginning. However, the payout could accelerate as the company makes increasingly bigger profits over time. Then we have those shares that are neither generous payers nor very fast growers. But they still pay us something.

In the next three chapters, we will look at some simple ways to help us identify good income, growth, and value shares. There will be a checklist of things to help guide us to make the right choices.

It is not necessary for a share to tick every box. It's great if it can do that. But even if it does, there is still no absolute certainty that the share won't fail. There is, unfortunately, no formula that we can apply that will guarantee success every time. But it is better to be roughly right than totally wrong.

What's a good income share?

Income shares are specifically chosen for their ability to produce lots of dividends over a sustained period. So, does that mean that a share that could promise to deliver oodles of dividends for every dollar that we use to buy it be a good income share?

The answer is both yes and no. Here's why.

A common mistake that many investors make when looking for good income shares is to focus too much solely on the yield. The dividend yield is measured by dividing the latest dividend per share by the prevailing share price.

We can find dividend yields quoted on numerous financial websites, or in the finance section of many newspapers. A quick trawl will give you a good feel for the average dividend yield in a particular market. It will also reveal those shares that either have excessively high or abysmally low dividend yields.

So, a share, which last paid an annual dividend of four cents, that costs $1 a pop would have a dividend yield of 4%. A $1 share that last paid two cents in annual dividends would have a dividend yield of 2%, and a $1 share that last paid an annual dividend of eight cents would have a dividend yield of 8%.

Which of the three shares is the best investment?

On paper, 8% is higher than 4%, which is higher than 2%. But what if we discover that the share with the 8% yield cost $2 rather than $1 just a few months earlier. Put another way, the only reason that it is yielding 8% rather than 4% is because the share price has halved.

The market could be worried that perhaps something might have gone wrong at the company. Maybe, investors think that the dividend could be cut. Then again, maybe there is nothing for us to worry about at all.

The upshot is that a high yield can sometimes be a sign of trouble rather than a sign of strength. Consequently, the dividend yield, whilst important, on its own doesn't always tell us the whole story.

How to find good income shares

If the dividend yield is not a good indicator, then what is?

Nobody ever said that the dividend yield is completely irrelevant. But it is just one of a few things that we need to look at. Finding good income shares requires a bit more digging around than simply running our fingers down a column of numbers in the newspaper.

For instance, a company's track record can tell us lots. If a company has demonstrated a history of paying regular dividends, then it could be worth looking at more closely.

Some might say that past performance is not a good guide of the future. That's absolutely right. However, companies generally don't like cutting dividends unless they absolutely have to. It's almost an admission of failure by management when they have to pass on dividends.

Cash is King

There are some companies that have never missed a dividend payout for decades. What's more they have even been able to increase their payout year after year. A company that has successfully raised its dividend for at least 25 years is called a Dividend Aristocrat.

There is something very special about these types of companies. They tend to generate copious amounts of free cash. Cash, by the way, is not the same as profit. Whilst profit is undoubtedly important, it can also be manipulated. Cash on the other hand can't be easily faked.

So, we need to find out just how much cash has been generated by the business. We can find this in the cash flow statement. This together with the profit and loss account, and the balance sheet are the three most important pieces of financial documents that we need to look at.

Essentially, we are looking at companies that can consistently generate free cash flow, even after forking out on things like capital expenditure. A company can use this free cash to do a number of things. It could pay out the cash as dividends, it could buy back its shares, or it could decide to pay down any debt that it might have.

On that last point, we don't want to see a company take on too much debt. A bit of debt is fine. But too much debt could put the company in jeopardy if interest rates should rise.

There is another reason why debt is bad. Lenders or bond holders rank higher than shareholders. A company must therefore make sure that its bond holders are kept sweet, even if it might mean upsetting shareholders.

That is why cash is King. A company with plenty of cash can keep both its shareholder and bondholders sweet at the same time. And if we are the shareholders of a company, then we want to make sure that our dividends are never put in jeopardy.

Ideally, the free cash flow should be at least twice the amount of dividends paid. This should give the company enough room to increase its dividends, even when times might be tough.

What else to look for?

There is one other thing that that dividend investors need to look at when choosing income shares. It is the amount of profit that a company makes on the money that investors have put into the business.

It is called the return on shareholder equity. The return bit is easy to find in the profit & loss account. It is the also known as the net profit or bottom-line profit. It is what remains from the revenue that the company makes after all the costs have been deducted.

The shareholder equity is the part of the business that belongs to shareholders. It is what is left after the company's liabilities have been deducted from its assets. The equity is the bit of the business that belongs to shareholders.

So, the return on equity is the amount of profit that a company makes on the money that shareholders have invested in the business. It is normally expressed as a percentage.

Returns on equity can range from low single digits to very high double digits. A low number would imply that the business is not very good at generating profit on the money that shareholders have invested in the business.

A high number means that shareholders are raking it in. It is akin to running a company powered by rocket fuel.

Twist or stay?

In fact, we want the company to invest as much money as it can get its hands onto in the business if the return on equity is high. It would be like pulling the handle on a one-arm-bandit that pays out every single time.

This can pose a problem for the company's management, though. Should it even pay out any profit at all to shareholders when the money could be better used in the business? It is not an easy call to make. There are strong arguments on both sides as to whether a company with a high return on equity should pay dividends.

Thankfully, there is a middle ground. Generally, these companies will pay shareholders something, but still retain some of the profit for its own use. The amount that they retain can give us a valuable clue as to how quickly the dividends could grow.

If a company retains, say, 60% of profits, then that money could be reinvested in the business that might be growing at, say, 15% a year. It means that the reinvested profit could be used to grow the dividends at 9% (60% at 15%).

If it only retains 30% of profit, then the theoretical dividend growth rate could be 4.5% (30% at 15%). We should still get our dividends either way. But it depends on whether we prefer a lot of money now or later.

Some businesses are required to pay out at least 90% of their income as dividends. They belong to a special category of companies known as Real Estate Investment Trusts or REITs.

They don't tend to grow quickly, but they can still throw off lots of dividends. They don't really have much of a choice. That's because they aren't required to pay much in taxes to the taxman.

But in exchange for the favourable tax treatment, they have to pay out most of their profit as dividends to shareholders.

CHAPTER SIX

Stock picking made easy - REITs

> *I told my mother-in-law that my house was her house, and she said, "Get the hell off my property."* (Joan Rivers)

No discussion about income shares would be complete without a nod in the direction of real estate investment trusts or REITs.

REITs invest in income-generating properties. They might invest in shopping malls, commercial offices, serviced residences, nursing homes, student lodgings, hospitals, data centres, industrial parks, car parks, and logistics facilities that are rented out. Some even invest in telecommunication towers.

These assets generate rental income, which, in turn, are used for rewarding investors with a share of that cash flow known as distributions. When we invest in a REIT, we are essentially landlords without the hassle that comes from dealing with tenants.

In effect, these distributions are a share of the profit that REITs have derived from their property. Distributions are, to all intents and purposes dividends, which mean that REITs are nothing more than a type of income-generating shares.

Confusion reigns

The potential for confusion about REITs lies in the rules that govern the way that they operate.

Unlike shares, REITs do not have any discretion, when it comes to paying dividends. They are required to pay out at least 90% of their rental income as dividends to investors, whether they like to or not. There are no ifs. There are no buts.

By paying out almost all of their profits to shareholders, REITs are, in turn, afforded a favourable tax status. They are virtually exempt from paying any corporation tax. It might sound a little too good to be true. But there is a reason for the taxman's generosity. REITs were created to solve a knotty problem over a shortage of property development.

A potted history

REITs were first introduced in the US around 50 years ago to encourage investors to pool their money to develop much-needed property in the market. The idea caught on in other countries later on.

Thing is, developing property on a massive scale can be costly. Very costly. But if property investors were taxed once at the corporate level and again at the personal level when they received their dividends, who would want to do it?

The answer in all probability is not that many. It would be far better for the investor to just buy an existing property, then rent it out, and pay any tax that is due on the rental income. That is precisely what buy-to-let landlords do.

But if we want property development on a massive scale, then buy-to-let doesn't quite deliver the goods. However, a favourable tax treatment through REITs might just do the trick.

So, REITs, with their favourable tax status, provided developers with the capital they required to build more. Meanwhile, towns and cities benefitted from much-needed construction.

That is primarily why REITs came into existence. But a REIT would only receive the preferential tax treatment if it was obliged to pay out nearly all its income as distributions to investors.

So, the attraction of REITs lies in their ability to generate long-term rental income for shareholders, who are also known as unit holders. These investors buy REITs for both the steady recurring income and any price appreciation, should the properties held by REITs increase in value over time.

Show me the cash

The income-producing characteristics of REITs can result in some curious but interesting features for investors.

Since payouts might be thought of as being somewhat predictable, REITs are often seen as proxies for bonds. In other words, they, like bonds, could be capable of delivering dependable income for investors, over the long term.

But just as bond prices might move in the opposite direction to interest-rate movements, the price of REITs have a tendency to do the same, also.

When interest rates rise, investors would probably want to pay less for each unit of a REIT to generate a comparable return from, say, a risk-free investment such as money in a savings account or a bond. Similarly, when interest rates fall, investors might be prepared to stump up more to capture every dollar of a REIT's distribution.

There is another reason why REIT prices might move in the opposite direction to interest rate movements. That is because REITs tend to borrow money to buy property. So, higher interest rates could result in heftier interest payments, which, in turn, could sap distributions available to investors.

The prospect of lower distributions in the face of rising interest rates could, therefore, depress the share prices of REITs.

Here's the rub

But there's a rub. Rising interest rates - rather than hurting REITs – could even benefit them.

Interest rates generally rise because the rate of inflation could be on the increase. So, in order for central banks to keep a lid on inflation, they need to ensure that their interest rates are high enough to bear down on rising consumer prices.

But in an inflationary environment, REITs could justifiably charge higher rents, which could result in more rental income and, in turn, deliver higher distributions to shareholders.

Put another way, REITs are a function of both prevailing credit conditions and the economy. We should try to keep that in mind when we are thinking about investing in REITs.

In theory, as long as one of those two things, namely, readily available credit or that the economy, is doing well, then REITs should be capable of doing well, too. In other words, they should continue to deliver income to investors.

With income from REITs as the primary objective for investors, it is perhaps understandable why there could be a strong focus on their yields. That is not an altogether wrong way to think about REITs. But it is not entirely correct, either.

Nevertheless, it can be as good a place as any to start looking for suitable REITs.

Cash is king

Distributions by a REIT have to be paid from income. So, it is crucial that anything that is paid out to shareholders is adequately covered by profits.

It stands to reason that the higher the distribution coverage, the better and safer it could be for us. It means that the REIT does not have to scratch around too hard to meet its obligations to shareholders.

Typically, dividend coverage of around two times profit for most shares is desirable. It allows the company to retain some of the profits to grow the business. But REITs are different.

They are required to pay out most of their income as dividends to qualify for the favourable tax treatment. Them's are the rules. So that's why the dividend coverage for REITs is much lower.

Consequently, profits are not a reliable way to look at REITs. No, they definitely are not. There are much better ways to gauge the health of REITs and their payouts. More about that in a minute.

Interesting times

REITs will typically borrow heavily to fund their purchase of income-generating properties. So, it is important to ensure that not only are dividends adequately covered but that interest payments can be easily met by the REIT, also.

We would probably want to see those interest payments covered more than three times by profits. The last thing we want to see are bailiffs knocking on the door because a landlord can't meet his financial commitments to the bank.

Those that can comfortably pay their interest bills might even be able to borrow more. But some countries have put a ceiling on the amount of money that REITs are allowed to borrow. That is sensible. But there needs to be a fine balance between borrowing too much and not borrowing enough.

Less may not be best

There are a couple of implications to the assumption of debt. And it may not always be the case that a lower level of borrowings is necessarily better.

Debt, if used judiciously, could significantly improve shareholder returns because the business is using other people's money, rather than shareholder funds to partially finance the business.

But too much debt could also be detrimental. Oh yes it can.

It can restrict the amount of money that a company could borrow at a later date to pay for new acquisitions. When that happens, the REIT might have to pass around the begging bowl for more money.

Debts also need to be either repaid or refinanced when the loans mature. There are no guarantees that either of those two things could happen, when the lender comes a knocking. So again, a heavily-indebted REIT might have to tap shareholders for cash.

By the book

We should never lose sight that REITs are ultimately property assets. So, it is important to think of them as such. We should weigh up carefully how much we are paying for every dollar of net asset behind each REIT.

In the same way that you would probably balk at overpaying for a house or a condo, the same goes for buying into a REIT. They are, after all, just a collection of income-generating bricks and mortar.

One way to value REITs is to look at their book values. The book value, or net asset value, is simply what remains after total liabilities are deducted from total assets. Since the properties held by REITs are valued regularly, the book value should provide us with a reasonable gauge of the underlying value of the REIT.

Sometimes investors are willing to pay a premium for the assets. At other times, the assets are trading at a discount. There could be valid reasons why the market might be either overly optimistic or downright pessimistic about a REIT.

An economic slowdown could make some properties less valuable. Remember the market is always looking forward to what it thinks might happen.

There might also be perfectly good reasons why the market could be prepared to pay a premium for some REITs. Prize assets in prime locations are highly valued. They might also rise in value faster than other properties.

But the best time to buy a REIT is when the market is under-appreciating the value of its assets. In other words, the best opportunities could be when a REIT is either not trading at a massive premium or even at a discount to its Net Asset Value.

That could happen for all sorts of reasons. Let's not forget that irrational market behaviour is not uncommon in the stock market. It happens more often than we like to think.

Capitalisation Rate

There is no shortage of REITs that we can invest in. In fact, most major markets around the world have a decent collection of REITs that we can trawl through.

That said, a common problem with comparing different REITs is that it can be a bit like comparing almonds with pistachios. That is just nuts.

Is it really possible to compare, say, a REIT with prime properties in the Central Business District of London with another REIT that owns a portfolio of suburban malls in Singapore? Which is better?

It's not easy. But the capitalisation rate is an easy way of solving the thorny problem. It looks at the rate of return that a property company expects to achieve from its assets. It is effectively a measure of the annual rental income that a REIT generates from its properties.

Some REITs have quite a high capitalisation rate, whilst others are disappointingly low. So, which is better?

On paper it might seem like a good idea to choose REITs with high capitalisation rates. But it could also mean that the REIT might be charging tenants too much rent, which, in turn, could mean that the high income could be unsustainable over the long haul.

It could also mean that the landlord might have targetted riskier tenants. Alternatively, it might mean that the tenants have only signed short-term leases.

Unfortunately, there is no right or wrong capitalisation rate. But perhaps those that are clustered around the market median for a particular country could be seen as more stable for the long-term investor.

Putting it all together

We have looked at different ways of valuing REITs. But what - if any - is the best method to look at these income-generating assets?

Should it be the distribution yield or the price-to-book, both of which are easy enough to find? The answer is that everything should play a part when evaluating REITs. There are no short cuts. We should look at REITs from as many angles as possible.

But if we should put ourselves into the shoes of a property manager, then it is probably the capitalisation rate that will be paramount. So, perhaps we should be paying a bit more attention to that.

The capitalisation rate could play an important deciding role in the types of properties that a REIT might want to buy. It could also determine - to some extent - when a REIT might decide to sell an asset. It could even set a ceiling on the level of interest that a REIT can afford to borrow money at.

So, from an income investor's perspective, we should perhaps start by looking at REITs whose capitalisation rates are bunched around the median.

We should also be looking for REITs that have demonstrated a good track record of growing their payouts too. That could be a sign of good management. So, as a final test we could set a criterion of, say, four consecutive years of rising dividends. In fact, we can be as ruthless or as lenient as we like.

CHAPTER SEVEN

Stock picking made easy - What about bonds?

Gentlemen who prefer bonds don't know what they are missing (Peter Lynch)

We mentioned bonds in the previous chapter without going into too much detail about these financial instruments. So, what exactly are these things called bonds?

They are nothing more than loans to companies, governments, and non-profit organisations. There are four main features to a bond. The first is the nominal or face value of the bond, which is normally set at $1,000, $5,000 or $10,000. This is the amount of money that a government or company wants to borrow. The most common is a face value of $1,000.

The second is the coupon, which is the interest payable on the nominal value. So, a bond with a coupon of 4% will pay interest of $20 twice a year to the owner of a $1,000 bond.

The third feature of a bond is the duration of the loan. It is fixed at the outset. If it is five-year bond, then the loan must be redeemed five years after it was issued. In other words, the loan must be repaid in full after five years.

The fourth, and perhaps the most interesting feature of a bond, is that it can be bought and sold after it has been issued. In fact, bonds have existed long before shares ever did. What's more the market for bonds is larger than the stock market because governments around the world just can't stop borrowing money.

Are bonds a good investment?

Some investors love bonds, especially government bonds, because they are perceived to be safe. But the price for that safety is probably a lower return than from shares. If we are happy to accept a lower return on our money, then bonds can serve a useful purpose in our portfolios.

We should, for instance, be able to work out to an accuracy of two decimal places how much interest we will earn from the time we buy the bond to the time when it is redeemed. If that is all that we want from an investment, then bonds are great.

Don't get me wrong, it is also possible to make money - lots of money - from bonds, if and when conditions are right. But first a quick look at how bonds can deliver a return for our portfolios.

If we buy a 10-year $1,000 bond that pays a coupon of 4%, then we can expect to receive $40 a year for a decade. But since bonds can be traded on the market, it means that we could either pay more or less than $1,000 for it.

So, we need to work out the return on the price that we pay for the bond rather than the face value of the bond. The arithmetic is not too difficult at all.

If we pay $1,100 for the $1,000 bond, then the average price of the bond is ($1,100 + $1,000)/2 or $1,050 because the value of the bond must eventually converge to $1,000 when it is redeemed.

Over the 10 years, we should have collected $400 in total coupon payments. But we will also have lost $100 or $10 a year because we had to pay more than the face value for the bond.

So, our effective yield if we hold the bond to maturity is ($40-$10)/$1,050 or 2.86%. It's not quite as high as the 4% that we were expecting. But that is because the market price of the bond changes according to prevailing interest rates.

Buy high sell low

Consider what would happen if the price of the bond should shoot up to $1,400. This time, the average price of the bond would be $1,200. The coupon would still be

$40 a year. But we would lose $400, or $40 a year over 10 years, when the bond is eventually redeemed.

So, our yield to maturity would be ($40-$40)/$1,200 or a big fat zero. It would be even worse if we had paid more than $1,400 for the bond. The yield to maturity would be negative.

We may be wondering why anyone would invest in a bond that is guaranteed to lose money? It's a perfectly valid question.

It will only make sense if we believe that interest rates could drop to below zero, which can happen in extremely bad economic conditions. It happened during the great financial crisis.

That provides us with a useful clue as to how some people might profit from bonds, namely, to buy them when we think that interest rates might be cut.

There is, if you haven't already worked out, an inverse relationship between bond prices and interest rates. When interest rates go down, bond prices generally go up. When interest go up, bond prices generally go down.

Consequently, bonds could be an attractive proposition when prevailing interest rates are high, and their prices are low. So, as interest rates start to come down, the prices of bonds start to rise. However, the question we need to ask ourselves is how high is high, and how low is low.

Economists spend inordinate amounts of time poring over data, charts and graphs, and statistics in an attempt to second-guess the possible direction of interest rates. As much as they would like to think that they know, they get it wrong more often than they get it right.

So, before we invest in a bond, we should ask ourselves if we are happy with a regular and fixed payout over the lifetime of the bond. If so, then investing in bonds can make perfect sense.

CHAPTER EIGHT

Stock picking made easy - Growth shares

"Anyone who believes in indefinite growth in anything physical, on a physically finite planet, is either mad or an economist" (Kenneth Boulding)

Growth shares specifically refer to companies that can grow their profits at a much faster rate than the market average. If on average, companies grow their profit at around 10% a year, then growth companies could see their earnings jump 30%, 40% or maybe even double every year.

Question is why don't we just shovel everything we have into these supposedly extraordinary growth shares? Surely, that is how we can make lots of money very quickly from the stock market.

That's an excellent point. But before we delve deeper into growth companies, here's a popular riddle about an amoeba in a jar.

The amoeba theory of investing

If an amoeba in a jar doubles every second, how long did it take for the jar to be half full, if the jar was completely full in a minute? That is all the information we have to work with.

The answer is 59 seconds because one second after that, the amoebas would have doubled again to fill the jar. What does that have to do with growth shares?

Growth companies don't operate in a vacuum. They function in a finite world. And in a finite world, there are limits and boundaries. There could be, for instance, a limit to the size of the market they serve. Hence the quote by economist Kenneth Boulding at the start of this chapter.

It is worth repeating the quotation because it is a common mistake that some growth investors make. They like to believe that growth is infinite. So, here is Kenneth Boulding's quote again:

"Anyone who believes in indefinite growth in anything physical, on a physically finite planet, is either mad or an economist".

It is undeniable that growth companies can expand their sales, and maybe even their profits at a fantastic rate. That is why the market loves them so much. But they don't exist in isolation. It is not unreasonable to expect competitors to want to offer similar products and services.

It happens all too often. Take a look at how many video-streaming companies that we can choose from today. It wasn't that long ago when there was just one. Today we are spoilt for choice.

Look at how many electric vehicles we can choose from today. There was a time when there was just one. What about ride-hailing companies? What about food-delivery outfits? What about online retailers? What about fintech companies that offer cross-border money-transfer services?

So, the market is far from boundless, limitless, and infinite, as many growth investors sometimes like to think. The reality is that growth could slow, if not come to a grinding halt. Exactly when that can happen is where our amoeba in a jar comes in.

Remember these companies are growing at the rate of knots. So, growth could come to a juddering halt just moments before market saturation is reached. Until that happens though, investors are prepared to pay handsomely for the projected growth. But just beware.

The next big thing

Some investors might be prepared to pay 10, 20, 30, 40, or maybe even hundreds of dollars for every dollar of profit that these companies are making. That is assuming that they even make any profit at all.

In some cases, they - by virtue of the fact that these companies are just starting up - are valued based on what they might turn into one day, rather than what they are right now. So, investors are effectively projecting long into the future the kind of rapid growth that these companies are enjoying today.

In most cases, the projections can be overly optimistic, with more hope than reality baked into the share price. And when disappointment sets in, so too do those lofty share prices that can sink faster than a hot soufflé meeting a blast of cool air.

It doesn't always mean that something terrible has happened at the growth company. It just means that it is not going to grow nearly as quickly. Consequently, it is not going to be quite as exciting as an investment. In other words, it has probably turned into one of those boring income share.

Old soldiers never die

There is an old refrain that says, "old soldiers never die, they just fade away". That is what can happen to those growth shares that turn into ex-growth shares.

Before that happens, they can still play an important role in our portfolios. They can provide the oomph that income shares are rarely able to do.

Think of them as the 100-metre specialist, Usain Bolt, of the portfolio, whilst marathon runner, Mo Farrah, could be our reliable income stalwart. They are both outstanding athletes in their own special way.

They perform useful functions. But we would never expect Usain Bolt to run and win a marathon. Nor would we expect Mo Farah to perform well in a 100-yard dash. However, we should be prepared to recognise them for what they are and what they do well in. We should be prepared to pay up for growth.

In the case of these growth shares, we can look at how much we are paying for every dollar of earnings they make. Let's say the going rate is $40 for every dollar of annual profit the growth company makes. This is generally referred to as a price-to-earnings ratio or a PE ratio of 40.

Is that expensive? It probably is, if we are only paying around $20 or less for every dollar of profit that other shares make in the market. Many financial websites will provide average PE ratios for various markets.

So, we can agree that a PE of 40 is probably quite expensive. But what if we find out that this company is capable of doubling its profit every year. So, the $1 profit it makes now could grow to $2 next year, and $4 the year after.

In other words, at today's share price, the PE ratio would be only 20 next year, and a PE of just 10 the following year. Would you still think that it is expensive? Probably not if the company can grow as quickly as projected. We might even conclude that it could be ostensibly cheap.

So, how do we decide if a growth share is cheap or expensive?

There is a rule of thumb that we can use. It even comes with a natty name - the PEG ratio, or the price-to-earnings-to-growth ratio. All we need to do is divide the PE ratio by the rate at which profit is expected to grow.

Anything less than one, could be considered cheap. A number around one is acceptable. But anything significantly greater than one could be deemed to be pricey.

So, a share with a PE of 40 that is capable of growing its profit 100% a year, would have a PEG ratio of 0.4. We should be doing cartwheels if we can find a share like that. But if it is only growing its earnings at 20% a year, then we might conclude that a PEG of 2.0 is not that enticing.

Show me more money

An attractive PEG ratio is one thing. But remember we want our portfolio to generate income, too. Consequently, our growth shares must also satisfy our need for regular cash.

A growth share that doesn't pay a dividend is about as useful to us as a teapot made from chocolate. If it can't show us the money, then we should be prepared to say thanks, but no thanks.

We shouldn't be too concerned if the dividend yield is low, though. After all, these companies need the cash generated to plough back into the business to make the business grow. But they must still be prepared to share some of the spoils with shareholders.

In the section on income shares, we looked at return on shareholder equity and profit retention. We can do the same thing here.

Growth companies tend to generate very high profit on shareholder funds. They also retain a lot of profit for use within the business.

That powerful combination of a high return on equity and a high retention ratio can turbo charge earnings growth and, in turn, deliver dividend growth. Put another way, annual dividends could grow 20% or 30% a year, which is virtually unheard of with income shares.

So, don't be too dismissive of a low dividend payout with growth shares. A one-cent payout that could grow 30% a year could double every couple of years. If the dividends can grow quickly, then so too could the share price.

Finally, the importance of cash flow should not be overlooked. When we were looking at income shares, we talked about why cash flow is crucial. It applies to growth shares, too. We need to ensure that there is plenty of free cash flow, and that any dividends paid out are adequately covered by profit.

CHAPTER NINE

Stock picking made easy - Value shares

"Better a diamond with a flaw than a pebble without" (Confucius)

We've looked at income shares, REITs, bonds, and we've also examined growth shares. It's now time to turn our attention to those mysterious things called value shares.

These generally refer to companies that have been punished by investors for one reason or another. Some might even go so far as to say that they have been unfairly punished by the market.

We can think of them as the Cinderella, the Snow White, and the Sleeping Beauty of the stock market all rolled into one. They have a hidden beauty that is just waiting for Prince Charming to come along on his white steed to awaken.

Point is, he may never arrive, or, then again, he could turn up as soon as tomorrow. We just don't know. If he does turn up, though, these value shares could be the belle of the ball, the star of the show, the talk of the town.

So, value investors need to have the patience of Job. Lots and lots of patience if they are looking for that fairy-tale ending.

Where did they go wrong?

Question is why are they unloved? Why has the market chosen to give these value shares the cold shoulder? Why can't investors see that these companies are truly beautiful beneath that temporary unattractive exterior?

It's probably for the same reason that Cinderella was banished to the kitchen, while her ugly stepsisters were enjoying their day in the sun. Poor Cinders found herself in the wrong place at the wrong time. Same goes for value shares.

Consider integrated oil companies. At one time they took pride of place in many investors' portfolios. Their share prices might have fluctuated with prevailing oil prices. But they were still remarkably popular.

Investors could almost count on these companies to send out dividend cheques at regular intervals. What's more, their payouts gushed like black gold out of a freshly-drilled oil well.

However, things changed as society took a dim view of industries that were not deemed to be environmentally friendly. Professional money managers dumped their shares to demonstrate their own green credentials. And so too did the share prices of these companies. A lead balloon doesn't even begin to describe what happened to their market values.

However, these companies still have intrinsic values, which is not the same as their market values. The market value is what investors think a company could be worth. Intrinsic value is what a company is actually worth.

When the market value drops below the intrinsic value, it could mean that investors have undervalued the business. They could be perfectly right to undervalue the business, which is why value shares can be quite speculative.

But if we are sensible in minimising the risk, then unearthing value shares can be quite rewarding. But to stress again, we must be patient.

Making sense of value shares

It is perfectly right to ask why value shares should even exist if markets are supposed to be efficient. It is a very valid question. One possible explanation could be that markets are not nearly as efficient as we are led to believe.

They are driven as much by emotion as they are driven by the fundamentals of investing. Fear of missing out

(FOMO) and you only live once (YOLO) can make people do some peculiar things in the stock market.

Fear and greed are powerful emotional drivers that can prompt people to buy and sell at the wrong time. Eventually, common sense will prevail. But the period between madness and when sanity returns is when value investors can find bargains.

Unearthing value

So, how can we minimise the downside? How do we know that we have found a lost masterpiece in a flea market? Here are four criteria that can help us find potential value shares.

The first is when the share is valued at less than two-thirds of the market average. If the market as a whole is prepared to pay, say, $21 for every dollar of profit that companies make, then put a tick next to a share if it is valued at less than $14 for every dollar of profit. In other words, if the PE ratio is less than two-thirds of the market average.

The next criterion is where the dividend yield is roughly similar to or more than the average for other companies in the market. Remember, after we have bought a value share, we are waiting for the market to discover it, too. It could take a while for that to happen. In the meantime, we want to be paid for holding the share.

The third criterion is when the share is trading below its tangible book value. This is arguably the most basic of intrinsic values. The book value is what is left after all the company's liabilities are deducted from its assets. If the company should go bust, then this is the residual claim that investors have on the company.

The final criterion is when a company has little or, better still, no debt at all. A company that doesn't owe anyone any money can't be forced into bankruptcy. It might be struggling, but it can afford to wait for things to turn around. It can't easily do that if debt collectors are constantly hammering on the door.

The outing

If you have picked a good value share, the value should eventually be recognised, if and when the right catalyst is in place. However, we have to accept that it could take a while. But that's alright, as long as we continue to collect dividends in the meantime.

That is why the value investor must be patient. That is not easy to do in a world where we have come to expect everything to happen at the click of a finger.

As Warren Buffett said: *"No matter how great the talent or efforts, some things just take time. You can't produce a baby in one month by getting nine women pregnant."*

CHAPTER TEN

Index trackers

"A journey of a thousand miles begins with a single step" (Lao-Tze)

By now, we should have the basic building blocks for putting together our portfolio of shares. This is merely a collection of stocks that should have a strong component of income companies, a modest collection of growth businesses and an optional sprinkling of value shares.

An often-asked question is why we should even bother building a portfolio of shares when it is possible to buy an entire market through a low-cost index tracker?

As the name suggests, index trackers are collective investments that mimic the performance of an index. The index could be the FTSE 100 in the UK, the S&P 500 in the US, the Nikkei 225 in Japan, the Straits Times Index in Singapore, or the Kuala Lumpur Composite Index in Malaysia.

In fact, there are trackers that track just about every stock market index in the world. There are even trackers that hold shares in companies from just about every part of the world, too. That's a lot of diversification without even trying.

Unlike a managed fund, there is no fund manager, as such, with an index tracker. The shares that are held through a tracker are the same shares as in the index. There is no one to decide if the tracker should hold more of this company or less of that.

That is why index trackers are cheap. And it is their cheapness that makes them attractive.

Reinventing the wheel

So, the question is why we should even bother trying to reinvent the wheel? Why would we even want to build a portfolio of shares when we can easily invest through an index tracker?

That is a good point. And in some cases, investing through an index tracker is probably good enough for some investors.

Within the index tracker, there could be a good collection of income, growth, and value shares. Each index could hold between 30 companies in the case of Singapore's Straits Times Index, and as many as 225 companies in the case of the Nikkei 225, and 500 separate companies in the case of America's S&P 500 index. That's a lot of diversification in one fell swoop.

In many cases, investing through an index tracker can be a really good place to start, especially if we are new to buying individual shares. The returns we can achieve will be roughly the same as the market return because these companies are essentially the market.

If the market goes up 8% in a year, then that is approximately what we will achieve through an index tracker, too. If it goes down 8%, then that will also be our return for the year.

What's more, most index trackers will allow us to make fixed regular payments that will get added to our existing units.

When the index is high, we will effectively buy fewer units with our fixed dollar of investment. When the index is low, we will get more units. It is called dollar-cost-averaging, which can be a powerful way to build our investments.

Lump sum or dollar-cost?

This brings us to an interesting topic of lump-sum investing. There could be occasions when we might come into a big sum of money, unexpectedly. It could be through an inheritance or perhaps we may have won the lottery. Question is how should we go about investing a lump sum?

This is when dollar-cost averaging comes into its own. Rather than investing a big chunk of money into the market in one go, we can spread it out over a period of time.

Problem with investing a large amount all at once is that we are fixing the investment at one point in time. But if we spread the money over a longer period, then some of the money might be invested when the market is high, and some could go in when the market is lower.

Tempting times

By committing to investing a fixed amount of money every month, we can also avoid the temptation of trying to time the market. Market timing can be very tempting. But there is well-trodden saying that it is time in the market rather than timing the market that counts.

It is only natural to sometimes think that the market can't possibly go any higher if it has already climbed steadily over a protracted period.

We may even be able to convince ourselves that the market is due for a fall. Consequently, we might think that it would be better to wait a bit before investing more money.

A bit can easily turn into a while, then it becomes a very long while because instead of falling the market just seems to defy gravity and keeps on rising.

What do we do then? Should we wait a bit longer or start buying straight away. Point is, wouldn't it have been better if we had simply admitted to ourselves that we just don't know?

There is something else for us to think about. A stock-market high today might not be a high in five-year's or ten-year's time. Remember we are going to be investing for decades. And over that time, there will most likely be many market highs and many market lows.

We might be lucky enough to get our timing right once or maybe even twice or thrice over that time. But we won't get it right every time. So, why bother trying.

CHAPTER ELEVEN

Building a portfolio with trackers

"Tell me and I forget, teach me and I may remember, involve me and I learn (Benjamin Franklin)

We are now at the point where we can start to roll up our sleeves and get to work on building our portfolios.

In the previous chapter, it was pointed out that starting with an index tracker could be a good place to begin. And it is. Through an index tracker, we will get immediate diversification.

Typically, trackers should have exposure to a wide range of companies in different sectors. These will generally include banks, insurers, telecoms, property companies, consumer-facing businesses such as supermarkets, consumer staples, consumer discretionary, perhaps some pharmaceuticals, and maybe some miners and farmers, too.

How much more diversification could we possibly want? The answer is probably not a lot more.

If we set up a regular investment plan into an index tracker, we should be able to gradually increase our holdings in a wide range of companies that could not only deliver capital growth but also income.

It is, without question, an effortless way to invest in the stock market. What's more, it can be quite cost effective, too. In general, index trackers are cheaper than managed funds. That is because there is no fund manager to decide what to buy, what to sell, when to buy, when to sell, and when to hold.

Instead, the holdings in the index tracker are determined by the composition of the index. So, the index tracker must simply follow what the market has decided.

It is even possible to invest in a number of index trackers. If we think that the FTSE 100 tracker doesn't provide quite enough exposure to, say, Japan, then we could invest in a separate index tracker that does precisely that.

If we would like to have some exposure to China or India, we could do that, too. There are trackers that follow the largest companies on the Shanghai and Mumbai stock exchanges.

What about a bit more technology, even though we might not always know our SAAS from our telco? That's not a problem, either. A tracker that mimics the Nasdaq should do nicely, if all we want is exposure to a bunch of tech shares.

Index tracker plus a couple

Let's say that after investing through an index tracker for a while, we feel that we might be able to do better than the market. It can happen, especially when we start to get more interested and more confident about what is going on in stock markets.

We might think that if only we had bought this particular share, which is not in the index, then we could have beaten the market. Or maybe we might prefer a bit more income than the dividends paid out by our index tracker.

Those feelings are perfectly natural. It means that we are ready to progress to the next stage of our investing journey. It's a bit like first learning to swim with the help of water wings. We are bound to feel very safe with a couple of air-filled floats around our arms.

But eventually, we might believe that we should be able to swim better and faster without them. Same goes for investing. But we shouldn't ditch the index tracker entirely. Instead, we can supplement our portfolios with one or two shares that we have the highest conviction in.

Every little helps

We might decide to dedicate 90% of our portfolio to an index tracker and the other 10% to our chosen share. Let's say the index delivers a return of 8% a year, and our own selection delivers a return of 12%.

It means that 90% of the portfolio has returned 8% (7.2%) and 10% has returned 12% (1.2%). So, instead of an 8% return on the portfolio, it has improved to 8.4%.

If we can maintain that small level of outperformance, then a $100,000 portfolio could turn into $224,023 instead of $215,892 after 10 years. That's an improvement of $8,130 for just a tiny increase in the annual return.

But what if our personal picks don't perform as well as expected, which can also happen. Let's say it only delivered a return of 6%. Now, the return on the portfolio has dropped from 8% to 7.8%.

In both instances, the return on investment is still not a million miles away from the market return. But we have at least learnt a bit more about buying our own shares.

Over time, we could find that our own picks start to dominate the portfolio, as we slowly become more confident about adding shares to the portfolio. There's nothing wrong with that. There's nothing wrong with continuing to invest through an index plus a couple, either. It's our portfolio and we can do with it as we jolly well like.

CHAPTER TWELVE

Building the portfolio from scratch

"I am sitting in the shade today because someone planted a tree a long time ago" (Warren Buffett)

Some of us might prefer to build a portfolio without the help of index trackers at all. That is perfectly alright, too. It might feel a bit like jumping into a pool before we have learnt how to swim, properly. But if we start at the shallow end, and slowly work our way to the deep end then we should, in theory, be fine. We can always head back to more shallow waters if we need to.

Since we are planning to buy shares in around 20 different companies, the portfolio should have about 12 income companies, roughly six growth companies, and a couple of value shares. It's a good idea to identify what those companies are likely to be before we start. We can always change our minds later on.

We need to remember that building a portfolio is a marathon rather than a sprint. We will be adding money to the portfolio for many years. So, there is absolutely no need rush things.

Swiss cheese your portfolio

Start with populating the portfolio with some income shares. They tend to be less volatile, and they also pay a decent dividend regularly. We don't need to buy all 12 before we move onto the growth and value shares, though.

Buying around half a dozen income shares should be fine to start off with. Then maybe a couple of growth shares before going back to another income share. Then maybe one value share. Then a few more income shares. Eventually, there should be some of each share in the portfolio.

It's called the Swiss cheese technique. If you are familiar with Emmental cheese, you will also know that it is full of holes. Those holes, which are called eyes, are a key feature of the cheese. It is what makes Emmental cheese, Emmental cheese.

Emmental cheese is normally served in slices. But if we randomly layer the slices on top of each other, the holes are no longer apparent, if we look through the stack of cheese slices. In other words, the once full-of-holes cheese has been transformed into a solid block.

Same goes for our portfolio. By slowly adding shares to the portfolio, we have effectively filled in the gaps to arrive at our desired pyramid of income, growth, and value components.

The Swiss cheese technique is not only useful for building investment portfolios. It can be applied to most projects that seem at the outset to be daunting and overwhelming. Just approach the task one layer at a time. Think of it as poking holes into the chore a bit at a time.

By taking small but deliberate steps every now and again, we can gradually move the components of an onerous task from the need-to-do list to the already-done list. Eventually, the entire task will be completed.

How much of each?

An obvious question at this stage is how much of each of our chosen shares should we buy for our portfolio?

We could, if we wanted, aim for an equal weighting for each share. In other words, 5% of each of the 20 stocks. But that would imply that we have no obvious bias or preference for any particular company. It can still be a good place to start, though.

Chances are we may like one particular share a lot more than another. Perhaps it is a company that we have particular knowledge about. Consequently, we may want the portfolio to allocate more than 5% of its cash to those shares.

We may think that a particular sector could do especially well. It is therefore understandable to want to have a bit more exposure to those types of companies.

However, we should try our best to maintain the overall shape of the pyramid. That is the first rule. Try to keep 60% of the portfolio in income shares, 30% in growth shares, and no more than about 10% in value shares. That is the principle of the pyramid technique - stability from the bottom up.

Within that strategic framework, we can still tactically change the allocation of our shares. A bit more here, and a bit less there. But try to keep any one allocation to below 10%. We don't want to end up having the tail wag the dog.

We have more than we think

As we gradually add money to our portfolio, something quite special and perhaps a bit magical can happen at the same time. Some of the shares that we have bought could already start to reward us with dividends.

Keep a note of the dividends that we receive but do invest them along with the money that we have earmarked at the outset to buy shares with. These dividends are ours. They are the fruits of our investments. But they are very different to the capital that we are putting into our portfolios.

It can be tempting to think that we can offset the money that we are putting into our salary-independence fund with the dividends that we have received. But that just means that we are effectively putting in less money into our portfolio. The only person we are deceiving if we should do that is ourselves.

Record keeping

It is vitally important to keep a record of money going in, money that we take out, and money generated by our portfolios. It will give us a good idea about how we are doing. There is a very clever function in Microsoft Excel that we can use to calculate how our portfolios have performed.

It is called the internal rate of return or IRR. Excel can calculate the return on our investments based on the cash that goes into and anything that we should take out.

When money is invested into the portfolio, it is represented by a negative sign. Don't ask me why. That's just the way it is. Whenever money is removed from the portfolio, it carries a positive sign. We can apply the IRR function by either using monthly cash flow or annual cash flow.

By knowing how much money we have put in, how much money we have taken out, and how much the portfolio is worth, we can use the IRR function to work out the rate of return.

Doing the calculation once a year is probably good enough. But it is entirely up to us if we want to do it more often. Just don't forget to convert a monthly rate of return to an annualised rate.

CHAPTER THIRTEEN

Rebalancing the portfolio

Life is like riding a bicycle. To keep your balance, you must keep moving (Albert Einstein)

Congratulations if you have reached this far. It means that we have understood the steps about how to build a salary-independence portfolio. We may have even started to build one already.

The good news is that the hard work is over. Now comes the fun part, which is to give the pot a quick but gentle stir every now and again. Try not to do it too often, though.

Running a portfolio can be a bit like cooking a pot of rice. First, we have to measure the amount of rice we need. That's not too dissimilar to working out how much we need for our salary-independence portfolio.

Next, we need to wash the rice carefully to get rid of any impurities. That's precisely what we are doing when we are sifting through our list of prospective shares for the portfolio.

After that we measure out the amount of water that we need to cook the rice. Not too much water because we will end up with a pot of slop if we are not careful. But not too little water, either. We don't want the rice to be too hard. Around one cup of water for every cup of rice, plus a little for luck will do very nicely,

So, the first thing we should try to maintain is the 60:30:10 rule. Take a look at the portfolio every now and again and make sure that the pyramid keeps its shape. But try to be reasonable. Don't freak out if the proportions deviate by a few percentage points here and there. Just make sure that it doesn't go too far out of kilter.

Remember that the growth shares will invariably accelerate faster than the income shares. At least we hope that they will. That is what they are supposed to do. Meanwhile, the income shares should spit out lots of dividends for us.

So, to maintain the shape of the portfolio, it is more than likely that we will be reinvesting most of the dividends into even more income shares. But which ones should we be adding more money to?

The choice is ours, entirely. Take a look at the ones that have the highest yields. After all these are income shares. Their job is to deliver income. So, highlight those that are not only the highest yielding, but are also able to sustain their payout.

At the same time, try to make sure that no single share accounts for more than around 10% of the portfolio. It really does help to manage the risk of putting too many eggs into one basket. No share is ever so good that it should totally dominate the portfolio.

Incidentally, we don't need to sell any share that should become too dominant. We can bring down their dominance simply by allocating money somewhere else.

Best made plans of mice and men

No matter how careful we are, things can still go wrong. But that doesn't mean we have done something bad. And it definitely doesn't mean that we should give up.

I remember an incident at one of Singapore's many food courts during the COVID-19 pandemic. It reminds me of how things can, through no fault of our own, go slightly awry.

At the height of the pandemic, dining in restaurants was strictly prohibited. But the draconian restrictions were relaxed when infection levels dropped to more acceptable levels.

One lunchtime, a family of three people managed to find a table at one of Singapore's popular food courts. Dad and daughter went off to buy food from the vast choice of food vendors. Meanwhile, mum stayed behind to sanitise the tabletop, and just about everything else in sight was given a good once-over, too.

Nothing was left to chance. The lady must have gone through three packs of disinfectant wipes cleaning not only the tabletop, but the table legs, the chairs, the chair legs, and the backs of the chairs, also.

When mum went to dispose of the spent wipes, a well-meaning food court cleaning lady appeared from nowhere and gave the table a quick wipe with her dishrag. The mum shrieked in horror. She shrieked a second time when she noticed that the dishcloth was a darker shade of brown.

It just goes to show that no matter how careful we are, we should still expect the unexpected. It might not be a conscientious food-court cleaning-aunty with a dirty dishcloth. It could be something far worse. It can happen very suddenly.

When a crash happens

Thing is, stock markets have a terrible habit of delivering surprises. For instance, day-to-day fluctuations in share prices are part and parcel of investing in the stock market. We just need to get used to them.

Sometimes, those fluctuations might affect individual companies. It could affect certain sectors. But occasionally it could affect the entire market.

When share prices thrash around violently, we say that the market is volatile. Amusingly, some people say that volatility is bad.

Ironically, when share prices rise as a result of the volatility, they think that it is not only fine and acceptable, but good to the point of being fantastic. However, when share prices drop, then they say that volatility is bad. We can't have it both ways.

Volatility when investing in shares comes with the territory. If we can't stomach sudden movements in share prices, then we might have to admit that investing in shares is not right for us. There is no shame in that.

Tough love

A 10% drop across an entire market from a recent high is known as a correction. It means that investors collectively think that the market might have become a bit too optimistic and that share prices might be frothier than a Starbucks cappuccino.

Consequently, they have decided to blow off some of the froth by selling some of their shares.

When the market falls by more than 20% from its most recent high, then it is known as a crash. It sounds much more dramatic than a correction, and it probably is. But whilst these types of movements are unpleasant, they are also not that unusual.

Between 1968 and 2020, America's S&P 500 index has fallen by more than 10% on 28 separate occasions. It has dropped by more than 20% on seven occasions. So, over the 52-year period, a correction has happened once every two years. A crash has happened once in seven years.

Put another way, we don't need to be a genius to predict a correction. We have a 50-50 chance of being right if you just make the same call every year.

The fascinating thing about a crash is that we wouldn't even have one unless the stock market has risen. So, nobody should ever be that surprised when the market drops from a recent high.

Just think about it. If the market never drops, then everyone would pile in to buy shares. It stands to reason. When that happens though, the market would become so ridiculously expensive that some investors would no longer be interested in buying shares.

When there is a dearth of buyers, then share prices will fall until they become cheap enough to buy again. Then we go through the wash-rinse-repeat cycle until we reach another high.

Take control

Point is, corrections happen regularly. Crashes happen less regularly but they still happen. However, we have no control over when they might occur. So, why would we want to worry about something that we have no control over.

It would be far better for us to focus our energies on looking at the things that we can control. So, what exactly are these things that we can control?

We can certainly control the shares that we want to include in our portfolios, which should be our main priority. We can also control how much of each share that we would like to buy.

Instead of worrying about market corrections, we should instead be looking closely at how the companies in our portfolios are performing. Are they consistently delivering higher profits? Have they been able to generate higher sales? What about those all-important dividends? Have they announced a hike in their payout?

Our focus should be on reaping increasingly higher income from our investments. We can't easily do that if we become too fixated on daily share prices and the collective value of our portfolios.

Warren Buffett once said that investing is about working out the yield on an asset over the lifetime of the asset. In other words, it is about how an asset could reward us over the long term. Over that protracted period, we may experience many market corrections and perhaps a few market crashes. But the company should still be able to perform, regardless of what is happening to its share price.

Instead of fearing those events, we should be exploiting them to their fullest. Provided nothing has changed at the companies we invest in, we should be taking advantage of those lower share prices to buy more of what we like.

In time, we might even learn to celebrate corrections and crashes. When that day arrives, we will then know that we have graduated from being a stock-market speculator to being a proper stock-market investor.

CHAPTER FOURTEEN

The finishing line

If I'd had some idea of a finish line, don't you think I would have crossed it years ago - Bill Gates

The day will arrive when all our hard work will culminate in a fully-functioning Salary Independence portfolio that will be big enough and robust enough for us to stop having to put any more money into it. In other words, we have achieved our dream of salary independence.

We could, if we want, continue to work to allow us to carry on adding more money to the portfolio. But we should always ask ourselves why we would want to do that?

It might be because we enjoy our job so much that we don't really want to stop working. Perhaps the job is so rewarding that to stop working could be more painful than carrying on working. There's nothing wrong with that.

When to call it a day

Some of us might enjoy our work to such an extent that the thought of not doing what we like doing would feel a bit like not filling in the final clue in a cryptic crossword, or not mopping up the last drop of gravy after a sumptuous Sunday roast.

The important thing to remember is that the objective of the Salary Independence fund is to provide us with choices. We can choose the time when we want to hang up our boots and call it a day. We can choose if we want to carry on working. We can choose if we only want to work part time.

Enough is enough

When that moment arrives, we can say enough to putting any more money into the portfolio. But there are still a couple of minor housekeeping chores that still need to be done.

The first is to maintain the overall shape of the portfolio. As we get older, we may not want too much of our portfolio devoted to growth shares. We should still have some growth shares, though. So, any spare cash could be used to buy more income shares. They tend to be considerably less volatile.

The second is to draw off 4% of the fund at the start of each calendar year. If the fund is worth $1,000,000, then take out $40,000 on 1 January.

Put that money into a bank account for living expenses during the next 12 months. And budget carefully. That is all the money that we are permitted to take out from the fund until 1 January the following year.

Remember, the drawdown limit is not a spending target. We don't have to blow every last cent just because it is there.

Another thing to bear in mind is that the value of the portfolio will vary from one year to the next. But it shouldn't swing around too much. Nevertheless, by taking the money out at the start of the year, it should let us adjust our budget for the next 12 months.

Another advantage is that it should give the portfolio a chance to grow during the next 12 months before we withdraw the next tranche of money.

The third housekeeping chore is that we can, if we absolutely need to, sell some shares to pay for our 4% drawings. But if we are shrewd, we may not need to sell any shares at all. Any dividends generated by the portfolio during the year can be set aside in readiness to fund the drawdown at the start of the following year.

After all, we should, after years of investing, have a fairly good feel as to when each of our companies will not only declare their dividends but also when they will pay them out. So, we should have a good idea about how much cash we could be collecting during the year.

Time to enjoy your life

With your Salary Independence portfolio in place, it is time to start enjoying the fruits of our hard work. But that doesn't necessarily mean that we should turn ourselves into couch potatoes. There is only so much television binge-watching that we can do.

Consider a hobby that you have always wanted to take up but maybe never really had the time to pursue. If you become especially good at your new interest, you might even look at ways to monetise it.

Have you ever considered writing a book? Maybe a novel. That's another way of generating a bit of extra income.

Are you any good at cooking or baking? You could put your skills to use by selling your prize marmalade through some local retailers. Maybe we could organise cookery classes? What about joining the gig economy? There will always be a demand for our skills.

Are you beginning to see a theme here? We're not talking about jumping on the treadmill or joining the rat race again. But it is never a bad idea to stay economically, physically, and mentally active, even if we have plenty of money in the bank.

It is always good to have a diversified income stream. But you probably knew that anyway. That's why we have a portfolio of income-generating assets. In much the same way, we can earn money in many different ways.

Just make sure that it is what you enjoy doing. You are now in the best possible position to find the right balance between living to work and working to live. That is what salary independence is all about.

CHAPTER FIFTEEN

50 dos and don'ts of the salary Independence fund

1. Do take a long-term view of investing.
2. Do resist the urge to buy on impulse.
3. Do pay off your credit-card bills in full.
4. Do compare what you spend today with your expenditure a year ago.
5. Do use the Rule of 72 when evaluating investments.
6. Do take your age into consideration when investing.
7. Do use the 4% rule to estimate the required size of your salary independence fund.
8. Do know the difference between the types of debt you have.
9. Do attend Annual General Meetings.
10. Do invest any dividends as quickly as possible.
11. Do make a list of at least 20 companies that you like.
12. Do consider the Rule of 100 when building a portfolio.
13. Do invest in what is right for you.
14. Do categorise your shares as income, growth and speculative.
15. Do fit your shares into the investing pyramid.
16. Do consider income before everything else.
17. Do consider cash flow as well as profit when assessing shares.

18. Do consider a company's return on equity.
19. Do make sure around 60% of your portfolio is invested in good income shares.
20. Do consider real estate investment trusts as an alternative to bonds.
21. Do keep a record of money going into and coming out of the portfolio.
22. Do buy more when a correction or crash happens.
23. Do monitor the income generated by the portfolio.
24. Do draw down 4% of the portfolio at the start of each year when you retire.
25. Do look for meaningful ways to enjoy your new-found freedom.
26. Don't invest with money that you will need within the next five years.
27. Don't ignore inflation just because it is low.
28. Don't bale out of the market just because it has fallen.
29. Don't do nothing with your cash.
30. Don't wait too long before investing in the stock market.
31. Don't start investing until you have a target to aim for.
32. Don't overtrade just because it is cheap.
33. Don't be afraid to speak up at AGMs.
34. Don't dismiss taking dividends in the form of shares.
35. Don't over-concentrate your portfolio.
36. Don't listen to pundits predicting stock-market crashes.
37. Don't try to time the market.
38. Don't follow the crowd.
39. Don't ignore a share that has a low dividend yield.
40. Don't invest in heavily-indebted companies.
41. Don't dismiss a low dividend yield too quickly.
42. Don't invest in value shares unless you are prepared to wait.

43. Don't ignore index trackers out of hand.
44. Don't rush to build a portfolio.
45. Don't forget to maintain the shape of the pyramid.
46. Don't panic when a correction happens.
47. Don't be fixated by share price movements.
48. Don't focus on things that you cannot control.
49. Don't spend more than the 4% drawn from the salary independence fund.
50. Don't forget to enjoy your new-found freedom.

Ingram Content Group UK Ltd.
Milton Keynes UK
UKHW040729260623
424053UK00001B/63